Guitar Chords Two
Barre Chords

Step-By-Step Techniques for Expanding Your Guitar Skills

MICAH BROOKS

© 2025 | WorshipHeart Publishing
All Rights Reserved.

Also By Micah Brooks

The Guitar Chord Collection Series:

Guitar Chords One: The Essentials:
Easy-to-Learn Guitar Chords and Techniques for Beginners

The Guitar Authority Series:

Worship Guitar In Six Weeks:
A Complete Beginner's Guide to Learning
Rhythm Guitar for Christian Worship Music

42 Guitar Chords Everyone Should Know:
A Complete Step-By-Step Guide To Mastering
42 Of The Most Important Guitar Chords

Fast Guitar Chord Transitions:
A Beginner's Guide to Moving Quickly
Between Guitar Chords Like a Professional

Guitar Secrets Revealed:
Unconventional and Amazing Guitar Chords,
Professional Techniques, Capo Tricks,
Alternate Tunings, Head Math, Rhythm & More

Guitar Chord Flipbook: An Essential Acoustic and
Electric Guitar Chord Reference Manual
that Fits in your Guitar Case

Ukulele Authority Series:

Ukulele In Six Weeks:
How to Play Ukulele Chords Quickly
and Easily for Beginners, Kids, and Early Learners

The Piano Authority Series:

Piano Chords One (All Seven Natural Keys):
A Beginner's Guide To Simple Music Theory
and Playing Chords To Any Song Quickly

Piano Chords Two (All Flat and Sharp Keys):
A Beginner's Guide To Simple Music Theory
and Playing Chords To Any Song Quickly

Piano Chords Three (Numbers):
How to Play Songs By Ear Without Sheet Music
Using The Nashville Number System

Piano Chords Four (Playing With Other Musicians):
Secrets, Professional Tips, and Methods for How to
Play with a Band, Team, and in the Recording Studio

Songwriting Notebook Series:

Blue Green Ombre Edition
Charcoal Edition
Fusion Coral Edition
Navy Blue & Gold Edition
Northern Lights Edition

Songbooks and Music:

Micah Brooks All Things New EP Songbook
Micah Brooks All Things New EP

Micah Brooks

Copyright Information

Published by WorshipHeart Publishing

© 2025 Micah Brooks Kennedy | WorshipHeart Publishing

ISBN: 979-8-9897924-1-2

All rights reserved. No part of this book may be reproduced or transmitted in any form or by any means, electronic or mechanical, including photocopying, recording, or by any information storage and retrieval system, without prior written permission from WorshipHeart Publishing. Violators will be prosecuted.

For written permission, contact WorshipHeart Publishing at: www.micahbrooks.com or email worshippublishing@micahbrooks.com

Cover design by Micah Brooks Kennedy

Dedication

I dedicate *Guitar Chords Two* to my new friends at ONE CHURCH. I am grateful to serve with you in worship and ministry, sharing the joy of music and the love of Christ. Your passion and dedication inspire me daily. Together, we are creating a vibrant community of faith and music. Thank you for welcoming me into this wonderful family.

Micah Brooks

Contents

Chapter 1: Welcome to Guitar Chords Two — 9
Chapter 2: The Key of F Essentials — 17
Chapter 3: The Key of B♭ Essentials — 29
Chapter 4: The Key of E♭ Essentials — 39
Chapter 5: The Key of A♭ Essentials — 51
Chapter 6: The Key of D♭ Essentials — 61
Chapter 7: The Key of G♭ Essentials — 71
Chapter 8: The Key of B Essentials — 81
Chapter 9: Final Greetings — 91
About The Author — 94
Connect With Micah Brooks — 96

Micah Brooks

CHAPTER 1

Welcome to Guitar Chords Two

Let's begin your guitar barre chords journey!

Welcome to *Guitar Chords Two*! Over the next few weeks, you will learn how to master barre chords. If you've heard that barre chords are complicated, don't worry. We'll work together to make learning them smooth and manageable. Once you know a few barre chord positions, the rest will be easier since they follow similar shapes. Let's get started!

What is a Barre Chord?

A guitar barre chord is a type where the guitarist uses one finger, usually the index (1), to press down multiple strings across the fretboard. This technique allows the player to play chords that are not restricted to the guitar's open strings, thereby enabling the playing of chords in different keys and positions on the fretboard.

In a barre chord, the index finger (1) acts like a movable capo, barring (pressing down) the strings across a single fret. The other fingers then complete the chord shape, which often resembles open chord shapes but shifts up the neck. For example, an E major chord shape can be moved up the neck with a barre to create F major, F# major, G major, etc. We will learn each of these chords and more in this book!

Barre chords are fundamental in guitar playing as they provide versatility and the ability to play chords in various keys without changing the guitar's tuning. They can be challenging for beginners due to the need for finger strength and dexterity, but they are crucial for advancing in guitar playing skills.

Why Play Barre Chords Instead of Open Chords?

Playing barre chords instead of open chords on the guitar offers several advantages, particularly in terms of versatility, range, and the ability to play more complex music. An open chord is one where some strings are not pressed down by any finger, making them typically manageable to play. Here are some reasons why guitarists opt for barre chords:

Key Versatility

Barre chords allow guitarists to play chords in any key, not just those easily accessible through open chords. This is crucial for playing along with songs in various keys or matching the key to a singer's vocal range.

Uniformity of Sound

Barre chords provide a more consistent tone as all the strings are fretted, which can be particularly important in certain musical styles or when striving for a specific sound.

Greater Range of Chords

With barre chords, a guitarist can play a broader range of chords, including major, minor, seventh chords, and more, simply by shifting the same shape up and down the fretboard.

Easier Key Changes

Transitioning between keys or playing songs with frequent key changes is more straightforward with barre chords, as it often involves moving the same chord shape to different fret positions.

Advanced Techniques and Styles

Certain styles of music and advanced guitar techniques rely heavily on barre chords. They are essential in genres like jazz, rock, and blues.

Fingering Efficiency

In some musical pieces, using barre chords can make the transitions between chords smoother and more efficient, as it can minimize hand movement.

Fuller Sound

Barre chords often use more strings than open chords, resulting in a richer sound that can be desirable in rhythm and lead playing.

Finger Numbers for Chord Diagrams

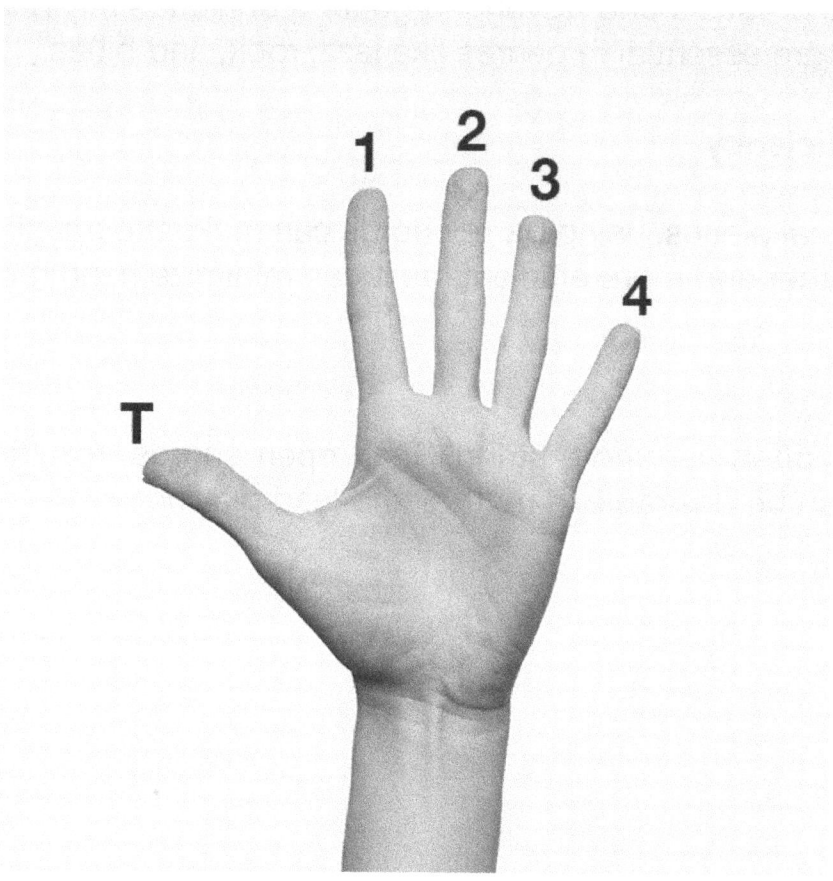

Though you may have learned the following about finger numbers and the explanation of chord diagrams in *Guitar Chords One*, it may be good to have a refresher before we begin. While you could use nicknames for each finger on your left hand (like index finger, pinky, etc.), most guitar teachers will use numbers for each finger. Numbers allows quick reference as you get into chord diagrams, transitioning, and barre chords.

Here are the details for each finger of the left hand (Left-handed guitarists will use the reverse hand, making this diagram opposite and for the right hand). The index finger is (1). Your middle finger is (2), ring finger is (3), and pinky finger is (4). The thumb is labeled (T). While you won't get into any thumb-playing in this book, you will in the following books.

Guitar Chords Two

Chord Diagrams Explained

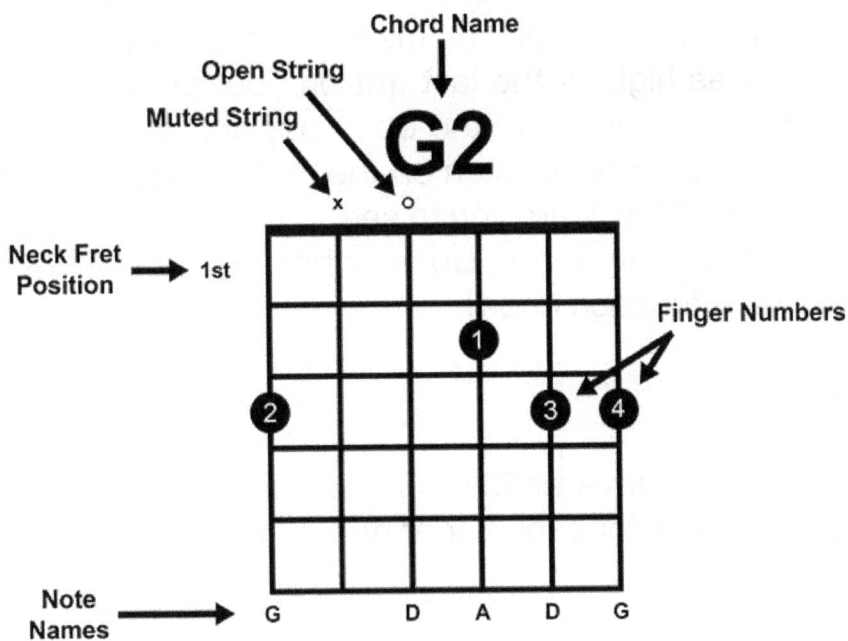

Chord Name

This section describes the name of the chord. This may include a chord suffix, like "G2", where the "2" is the modifier.

Open String

An open string is a guitar string played with no finger touching it. The note name is the string's name. For example, if you play an open fourth string, like in this "G2" chord example above, the open note being played on the [D] string is a "D".

Muted String

A muted string is either being muted by a neighboring finger or intentionally not played with the strumming hand. In this "G2" chord example, the fifth string [A] is not played.

Neck Fret Position

The neck fret position number is essential to always notice when reviewing a chord diagram. That number signifies the starting position of your fingers on the neck. It can go as high as the last fret on your guitar. If you see a "1st" denotation, the chord is played in the open position at the beginning of the neck. "1st" is the home base position on the guitar. Everything else is related to that home base position. Were you to see "3rd", like in a "C#m" chord, your root note begins on the fourth fret. Do your best to observe the indication of the neck fret position for each chord.

Finger Numbers

Reference the section above entitled *Finger Numbers for Chord Diagrams*. Note the specific number for each finger of the left hand.

Note Names

Below each chord diagram are the note names being played per string. Notice that these are not the root names of the strings when being played open. Instead, these are the notes being played after fretting the chord. Some of the notes will be open notes, but only when no finger is needed for that particular string in the chord. No note name will be present when a string is omitted or muted.

How This Book Is Set Up

When you learn barre chords, you inevitably learn many sharps (#) and flats (♭). The best way to make connections between the chords is to understand them as they relate to a key. So, this book begins with the Key of F, having only one flat note, B♭; thus, most chords are natural (such as C or Dm as opposed to B♭). As you progress throughout the book, you'll add one flattened note to each chapter. Adding the flattened note will teach you at least two new chords per key while building on the foundation of chords from the last key. The only departure from this plan is when you learn the chords in the Key of B (Chapter 8). In it, you'll learn the barre chords associated with a key built from five sharp notes rather than flat.

Now, onward to learning your first barre chords!

Micah Brooks

CHAPTER 2

The Key of F Essentials

Introduction

The first key to learn barre chords is the key of F. It's first because it only includes one flat note (B♭); thus, it mainly uses natural notes. If you were to learn the piano, it is one of the first flat keys to practice because it contains primarily white keys, with only one black key, known as flat keys. In this chapter, you will learn the F, C, Dm, B♭, and Gm chords. Additionally, you'll see both of the standard barre chord shapes you'll use throughout the rest of the book. There are also a few chord progressions to use as practice as you master these new barre chords. Let's begin!

Key of F: 1 Flat (B♭)

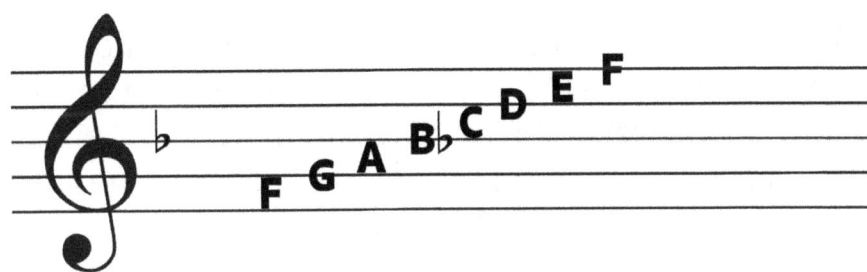

Essential Chords in the Key of F

F Chord

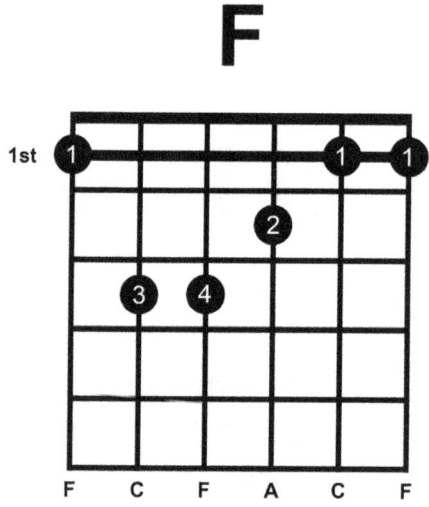

F Chord Information:
- Number of Strings Used: Six (6)
- Level of Difficulty: Moderate

Follow this fingering progression to play an F chord:

The first step is to lay your index (1) finger across all six strings on the first fret. You need to press down all the strings to hear each note. Now that you have the first finger in place add your ring (3) and pinky (4) fingers to the third frets of the fifth [A] and fourth [D] strings, respectively. Last, add your middle (2) finger onto the second fret of the third [G] string. Once all are in place, you can strum across all six strings and produce an F chord. The first few times you strum the F chord, you may have fret buzz or not be able to produce sound at all. This chord takes practice. To rehearse this, take your hand off the guitar, reposition it to form an F chord, and work to hear each note.

C Chord

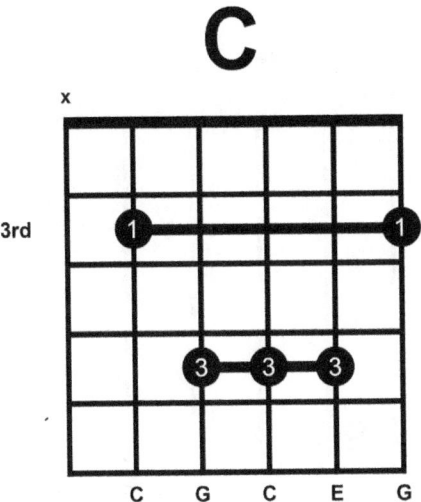

C Chord Information:
- Number of Strings Used: Five (5)
- Level of Difficulty: Moderate

Follow this fingering progression to play a C chord:

Start by taking your index (1) finger and lay it as flat as you can across the third fret of all five strings, beginning at the fifth string [A] all the way across to the first string [e]. You can omit the sixth string [E] for this chord. The last addition is your ring (3) finger laid across the fifth fret of the fourth [D], third [G], and second [B] strings. As in other chords like this, making your ring finger (3) lay flat across all three strings is difficult. You should not cover up the first [e] string currently being pressed down by your index (1) finger. You can now strum the last five strings to play a C barre chord.

Dm Chord

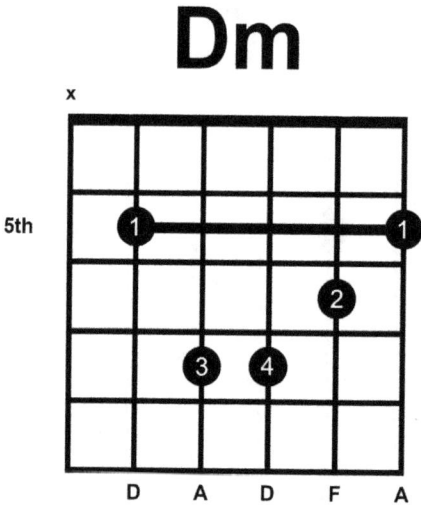

Dm Chord Information:
- Number of Strings Used: Five (5)
- Level of Difficulty: Moderate

Follow this fingering progression to play a Dm chord:

Lay your index (1) finger as flat as you can across the fifth fret of all five strings, beginning at the fifth string [A] all the way across to the first string [e]. Leave out the sixth string [E] for this chord. Next, add your ring (3) and pinky (4) fingers across the seventh frets of the fourth [D] and third [G] strings, respectively. Last, add your middle (2) finger to the sixth fret of the second [B] string. Strum the last five strings to play a Dm barre chord.

B♭ Chord

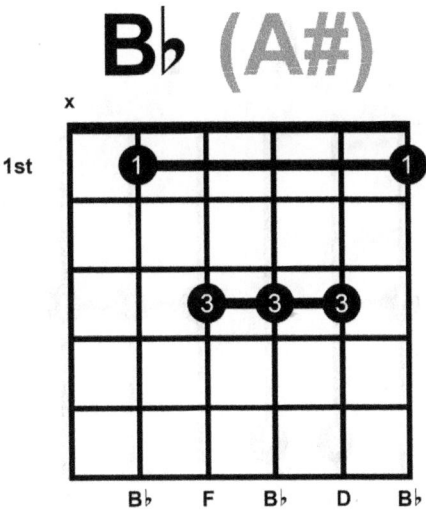

B♭ Chord Information:
- Number of Strings Used: Five (5)
- Level of Difficulty: Moderate

Follow this fingering progression to play a B♭ chord:

Lay your index (1) finger as flat as you can across the first fret of all five strings, beginning at the fifth string [A] all the way across to the first string [e]. You can omit the sixth string [E] for this chord. The last addition is your ring (3) finger laid across the fifth third of the fourth [D], third [G], and second [B] strings. You can now strum the last five strings to play a B♭ barre chord. Another name for B♭ is A#.

Gm Chord

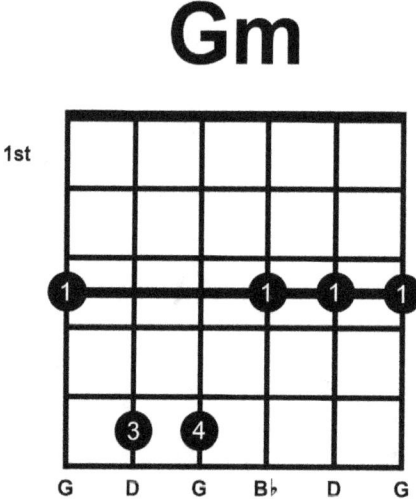

Gm Chord Information:
- Number of Strings Used: Six (6)
- Level of Difficulty: Moderate

Follow this fingering progression to play a Gm chord:

First, lay your index (1) finger across all six strings on the third fret. Then, add your ring (3) and pinky (4) fingers to the fifth frets of the fifth [A] and fourth [D] strings, respectively. Once in place, you should be able to strum across all six strings to produce a Gm chord. You must hear the third fret note on the third [G] string. As in the other six-string minor chords, that third fret note makes the Gm a minor chord and not major.

Practice

Below are some progressions you can try. Furthermore, you could create your own progressions. You can also move quicker between chords by making each chord two beats rather than four. Get creative!

|: F | B♭ | C | B♭ :|

|: F | Dm | C | B♭ :|

|: F | C | Dm | B♭ :|

|: F | Gm | B♭ | C :|

|: Gm | Dm | F | B♭ :|

|: F | B♭ | Gm | C :|

Chapter 2 Guitar Lesson

Barre Chord Root Movements: 6 String Barre Chord Shape

Forming barre chords is essential in playing in flat and sharp keys. Another benefit is the ability to move chords up and down the neck to swiftly change chords without needing to change fingerings. It's about changing the root note. For example, in this chapter, you learned the F barre chord and a B♭ that utilized a different chord shape. The way it is taught in this chapter, you would need to move your fingers from the sixth-string version of the F to the five-string version of the B♭. But there is another way you could move one chord to the other. The F chord begins with the index finger across the first fret. If you move all your fingers, keeping the same shape, up to where the index finger is on the sixth fret, you have created a B♭ chord. Check out the chord shapes below.

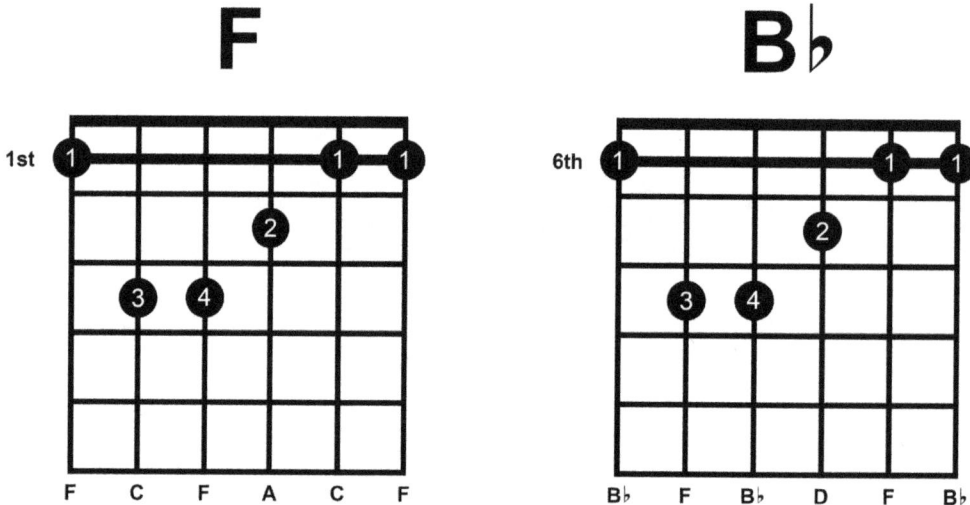

You could do the same thing to move to a C chord you did with the F to B♭ by moving to the eighth fret. Remember to keep your fingers on the neck of the guitar the entire time as you transition to each chord. You should slightly loosen the fingers as you move to be able to move quickly, then firmly place them down again when you reach your chord destination.

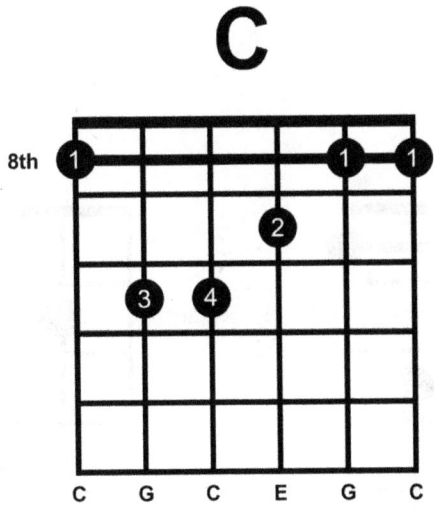

Now, move from F to B♭ to C and back to F. You will have a strong progression using only the six-string barre chord shape.

Barre Chord Root Movements: 5 String Barre Chord Shape

Much like the six-string barre chord shape, there is a standard 5 string barre chord shape. You've learned it earlier in the chapter with the C and B♭ chords. Let's move it up and down the guitar neck to create some progressions. Begin by learning this new F chord shape by moving the 5-string barre shape up to the 8th fret.

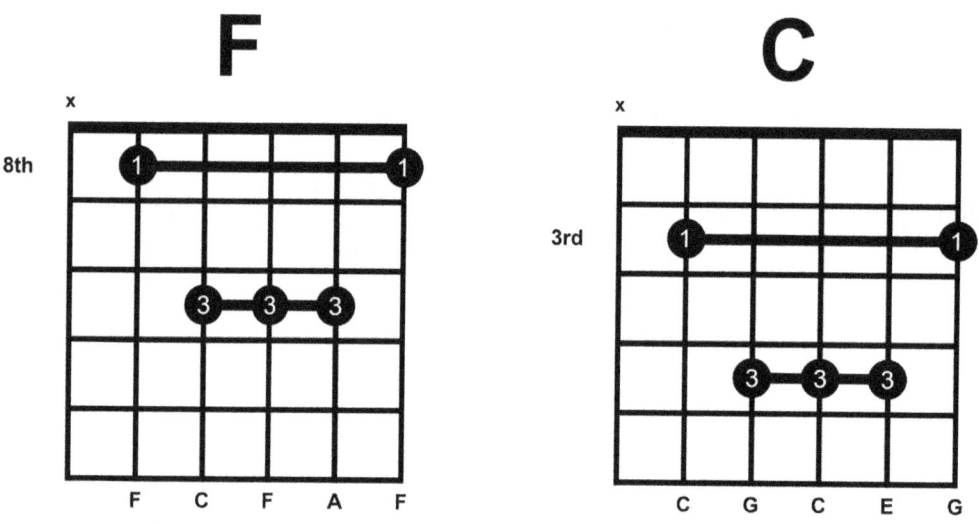

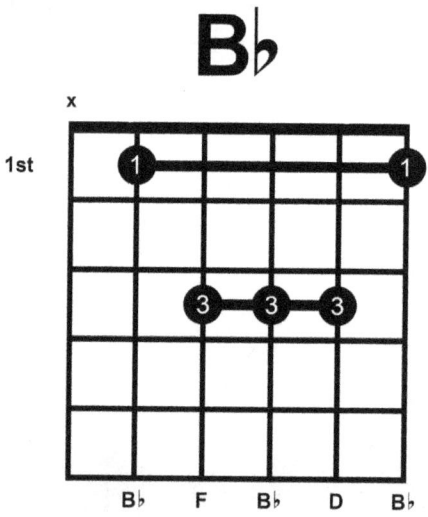

Summary

Throughout this chapter, you have learned five of the essential chords in the key of F. Plus, you now have the two standard barre chord shapes that will carry you through all the other chapters in this book. Next, we move on to the key of B♭!

Micah Brooks

CHAPTER 3
The Key of B♭ Essentials

Introduction

Welcome to learning the essential chords in the key of B♭. From the beginning, it is important to note that most of the chords in this key have two names, a flat and a sharp name. Typically, you will see these chords using their flat names; therefore, the flats are most prominent here. However, you should know both because you may encounter their sharp names from time to time. In this chapter, you will learn the following chords: B♭, F, Gm, E♭, and Cm. You'll notice that this key shares some of those in the key of F. It makes the two keys relative to one another but not the same. You'll also learn about the importance of muscle memory in the guitar lesson section. Finally, try out your new chords with some practice chord progressions. However, you can also search the internet for songs that use these chords. Let's get started!

Key of B♭: 2 Flats (B♭, E♭)

Essential Chords in the Key of B♭

B♭ Chord

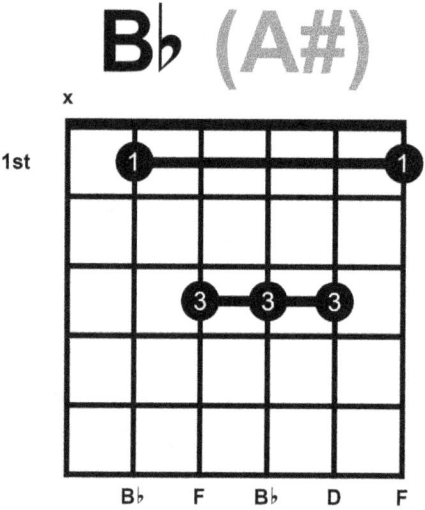

B♭ Chord Information:
- Number of Strings Used: Five (5)
- Level of Difficulty: Moderate

Follow this fingering progression to play a B♭ chord:

Lay your index (1) finger as flat as you can across the first fret of all five strings, beginning at the fifth string [A] all the way across to the first string [e]. You can omit the sixth string [E] for this chord. The last addition is your ring (3) finger laid across the fifth third of the fourth [D], third [G], and second [B] strings. You can now strum the last five strings to play a B♭ barre chord. Another name for the B♭ chord is A#.

F Chord

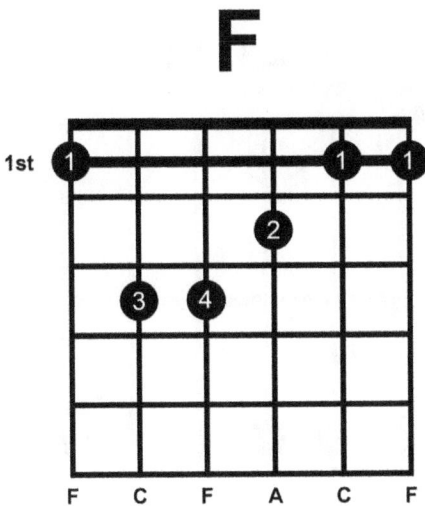

F Chord Information:
- Number of Strings Used: Six (6)
- Level of Difficulty: Moderate

Follow this fingering progression to play an F chord:

The first step is to lay your index (1) finger across all six strings on the first fret. You need to press down all the strings to hear each note. Next, add your ring (3) and pinky (4) fingers onto the third frets of the fifth [A] and fourth [D] strings, respectively. Last, add your middle (2) finger onto the second fret of the third [G] string. Once all are in place, you can strum across all six strings and produce an F chord.

Gm Chord

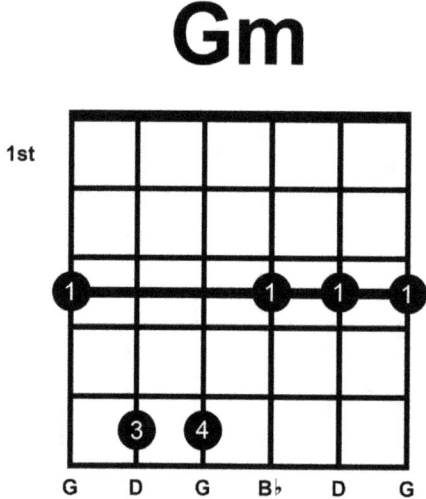

Gm Chord Information:
- Number of Strings Used: Six (6)
- Level of Difficulty: Moderate

Follow this fingering progression to play a Gm chord:

First, lay your index (1) finger across all six strings on the third fret. Then, add your ring (3) and pinky (4) fingers to the fifth frets of the fifth [A] and fourth [D] strings, respectively. Once in place, you should be able to strum across all six strings to produce a Gm chord. You must hear the third fret note on the third [G] string. As in the other six-string minor chords, that third fret note makes the Gm a minor chord and not major.

E♭ Chord

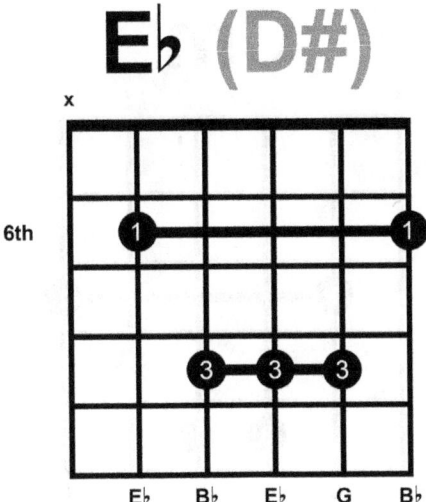

E♭ Chord Information:
- Number of Strings Used: Five (5)
- Level of Difficulty: Moderate

Follow this fingering progression to play an E♭ chord:

Begin by placing your index (1) finger on the sixth fret across the last five strings, omitting the sixth [E] string. Next, take your ring (3) finger and barre the eighth fret of the fourth [D], third [G], and second [B] strings. It is essential that you do not cover up the first [e] string that the index (1) finger is currently pressing down on the sixth fret. Strum only the last five strings, omitting the sixth [E] string to play E♭. Another name for E♭ is D#.

Cm Chord

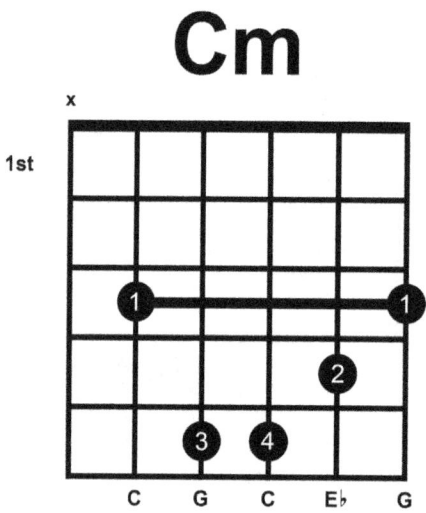

Cm Chord Information:
- Number of Strings Used: Five (5)
- Level of Difficulty: Moderate

Follow this fingering progression to play a Cm chord:

Start by taking your index (1) finger and laying it as flat as you can across the third fret of all five strings, beginning at the fifth [A] string all the way to the first [e] string. Next, add your middle (2) finger onto the fourth fret of the second [B] string. Last, add your ring (3) finger and your pinky (4) finger to the fifth frets of the fourth [D] and third [G] strings, respectively. Once all fingers are in place, you will strum the last five strings, leaving out the sixth [E] string not being pressed down to make a Cm.

Practice

You can use the following practice progressions to gain strength playing in the key of B♭.

|: B♭ | F | B♭ | F :|

|: B♭ | F | Gm | E♭ :|

|: B♭ | E♭ | F | Gm :|

|: B♭ | Cm | E♭ | F :|

|: E♭ | Cm | Gm | F :|

Chapter 3 Guitar Lesson

Building Muscle Memory for Quick Changes

Muscle memory is essential for many parts of life, especially in guitar playing. When you learn a chord, it builds a pathway in the brain. Practicing strengthens neural connections, causing muscle memory to develop. Once you have established the required connections for a chord or chord shape like we are learning in this book, you can transition smoothly and quickly between chords. Let's look at some exercises to build your chord muscle memory.

An excellent exercise is moving from your B♭ chord to the Cm. It allows you to slide up the neck of the guitar's two frets and forces you to move three of your four fingers from their positions on B♭ to make the Cm. I recommend strumming four times on B♭, then moving to Cm and strumming four. Repeat the process for a full minute then take a break. Do your best to keep consistent rhythmic timing. Even if you do not get all of your fingers perfectly onto the Cm chord, move back to the B♭ when the four strums are finished. As you complete this exercise over several days, you'll get better and quicker at making this transition, thus building muscle memory.

Another exercise you can practice is moving from B♭ to F. This is a solid progression to practice each day to build muscle memory as it utilizes two of the most important barre chord shapes. Much like you did with the B♭ to Cm, now practice moving between B♭ to F, strumming four times on each. Even if you haven't entirely transitioned before your four strums are completed, move back to the other chord. It will strengthen muscle memory even if there is some fret buzz as you transition.

Summary

In this chapter, you've learned the essential chords in the key of B♭. Also, you've learned the importance of muscle memory, which you will carry throughout the rest of this book. Remember, practicing a little daily is better than a lot once or twice each week, especially as you develop muscle memory. Now, let's move on to the key of E♭!

Micah Brooks

CHAPTER 4

The Key of E♭ Essentials

Introduction

Welcome to learning the essential chords in the key of E♭. You'll learn E♭, B♭, Cm, A♭, and Fm in this chapter. You'll also discover how to incorporate open and barre chords to create a unique blend of the two sounds. At the end of the chapter, there are some practice chord progressions to help you master each of the new chords. Let's begin!

Key of E♭: 3 Flats (E♭, A♭, B♭)

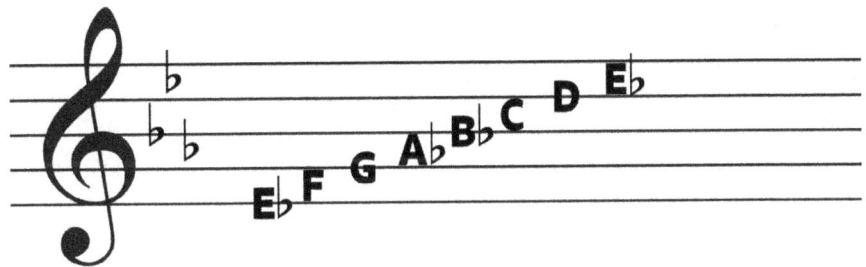

Essential Chords in the Key of E♭

E♭ Chord

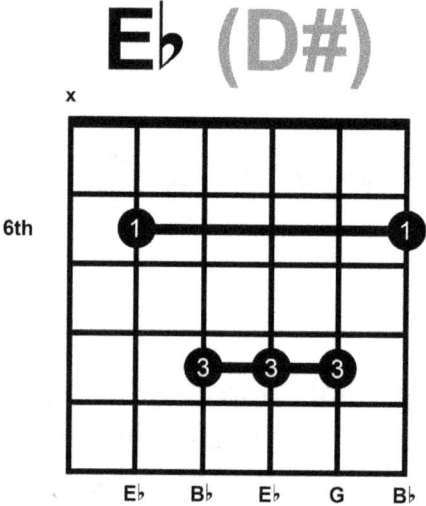

E♭ Chord Information:
- Number of Strings Used: Five (5)
- Level of Difficulty: Moderate

Follow this fingering progression to play an E♭ chord:

Begin by placing your index (1) finger on the sixth fret across the last five strings, omitting the sixth [E] string. Next, take your ring (3) finger and barre the eighth fret of the fourth [D], third [G], and second [B] strings. It is important that you do not cover up the first [e] string that the index (1) finger is currently pressing down on the sixth fret. Strum only the last five strings, omitting the sixth [E] string to play E♭. Another name for E♭ is D#.

B♭ Chord

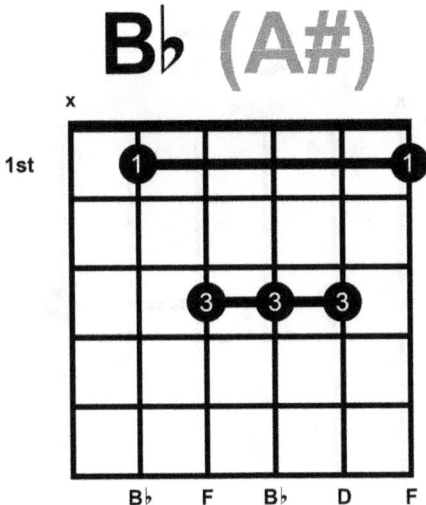

B♭ Chord Information:
- Number of Strings Used: Five (5)
- Level of Difficulty: Moderate

Follow this fingering progression to play a B♭ chord:

Lay your index (1) finger as flat as you can across the first fret of all five strings, beginning at the fifth string [A] all the way across to the first string [e]. You can omit the sixth string [E] for this chord. The last addition is your ring (3) finger laid across the fifth third of the fourth [D], third [G], and second [B] strings. You can now strum the last five strings to play a B♭ barre chord. Another name for the B♭ chord is A#.

Cm Chord

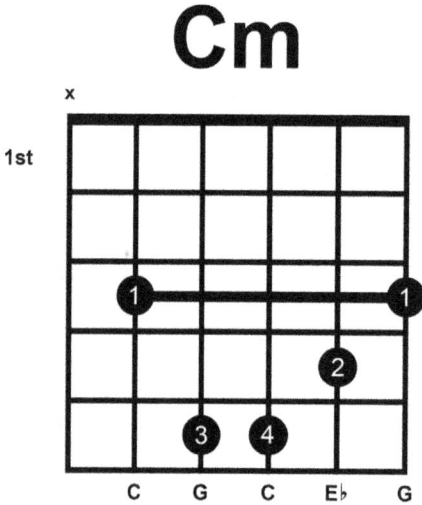

Cm Chord Information:
- Number of Strings Used: Five (5)
- Level of Difficulty: Moderate

Follow this fingering progression to play a Cm chord:

Start by taking your index (1) finger and laying it as flat as you can across the third fret of all five strings, beginning at the fifth [A] string all the way to the first [e] string. Next, add your middle (2) finger onto the fourth fret of the second [B] string. Last, add your ring (3) finger and your pinky (4) finger to the fifth frets of the fourth [D] and third [G] strings, respectively. Once all fingers are in place, you will strum the last five strings, leaving out the sixth [E] string not being pressed down to make a Cm.

A♭ Chord

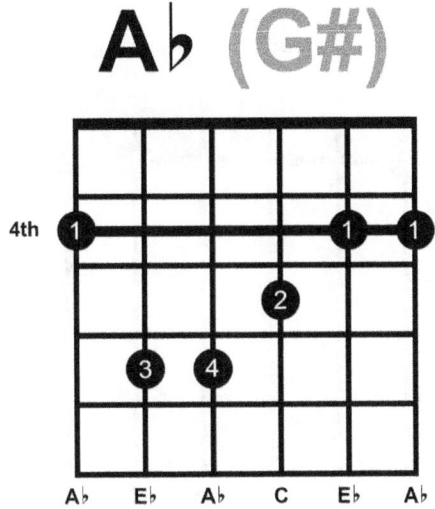

A♭ Chord Information:
- Number of Strings Used: Six (6)
- Level of Difficulty: Moderate

Follow this fingering progression to play an A♭ chord:

Begin by playing your index (1) finger across all six strings on the fourth fret. Then, add your ring (3) and pinky (4) fingers on the sixth frets of the fifth [A] and fourth [D] strings. Last, place your middle (2) finger onto the fifth fret of the third [G] string. Strum all six strings. Practice this chord to increase strength. Another way to say A♭ is G#.

Fm Chord

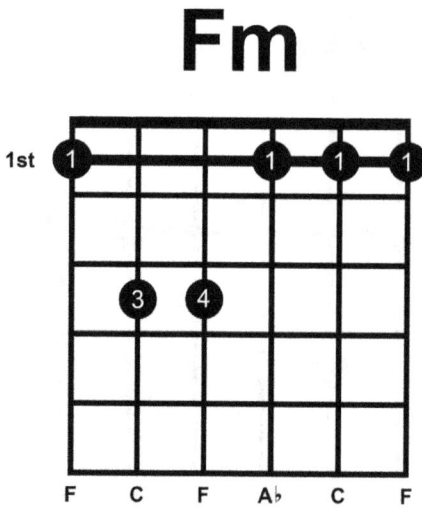

Fm Chord Information:
- Number of Strings Used: Six (6)
- Level of Difficulty: Moderate

Follow this fingering progression to play an Fm chord:

Begin by laying your index (1) finger across all six strings on the first fret. Next, add your ring (3) and pinky (4) fingers to the third frets of the fifth [A] and fourth [D] strings, respectively. Once each finger is in place, strum across all six strings to produce an Fm chord. Make sure to keep a strong barre on the first frets of the third [G], second [B], and first [e] strings. The minor note, "A♭", is created on the first fret of the third [G] string. Make sure you can hear that note.

Practice

Now, let's move on to some barre chord practice using the chords learned in this chapter.

|: E♭ | B♭ | E♭ | B♭ :|

|: E♭ | B♭ | Cm | A♭ :|

|: E♭ | Cm | A♭ | B♭ :|

|: E♭ | Fm | A♭ | B♭ :|

|: Fm | E♭ | Cm | B♭ :|

Chapter 4 Guitar Lesson

Incorporating Barre Chords into Common Progressions

Learn to apply barre chords within common chord progressions used in popular music. This will help bridge the gap between practice and practical use in performances.

In *Guitar Chords One*, you've learned the most essential open chords a guitarist needs. If you haven't read that book, find the description online and ensure you know the list of open chords before proceeding here. If any of them are foreign to you, consider purchasing that book, as you'll need to know those chords even more than the ones we are working through in this one.

Integrating barre chords with open chords is an excellent skill. An open chord is one played that includes some open strings as well as pressed-down frets. For example, a traditional G chord contains two or even three open notes. It allows the guitar to resonate more than barre chords, so they are often taught first. Here are some examples of using chords from Chapter One to practice integrating open and barre chords.

The first progression includes the barre chords F and B♭ while incorporating the open C and Dm chords. Using each shape lets you keep the fretting hand close to the guitar's nut, bringing a relative motion to the progression. You should notice continuity between them since several of the same notes will be in many chords.

Guitar Chords Two

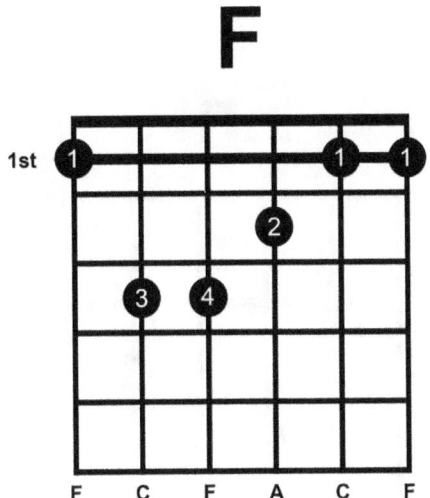
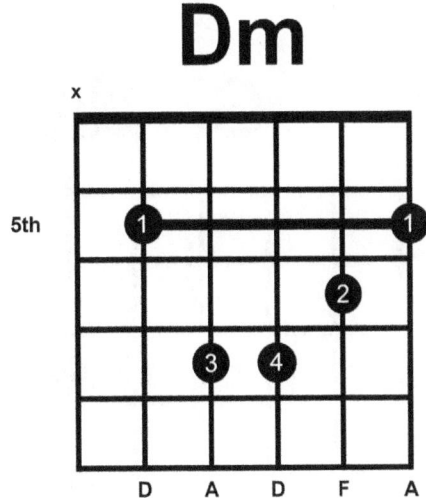
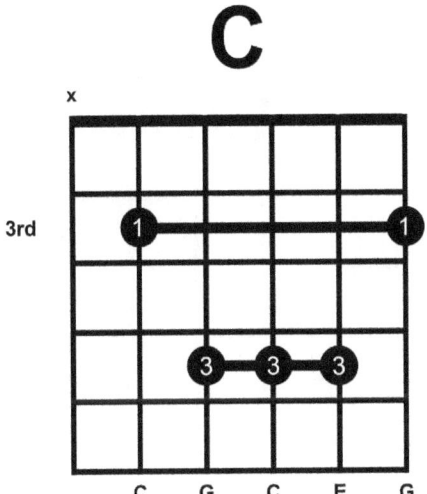
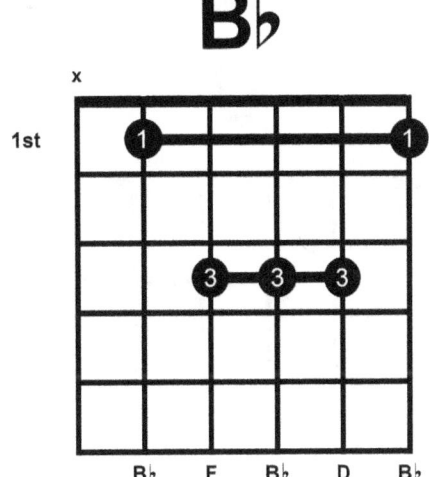

47

Another progression that marries barre with open chords is in the key of G. Try the following chords.

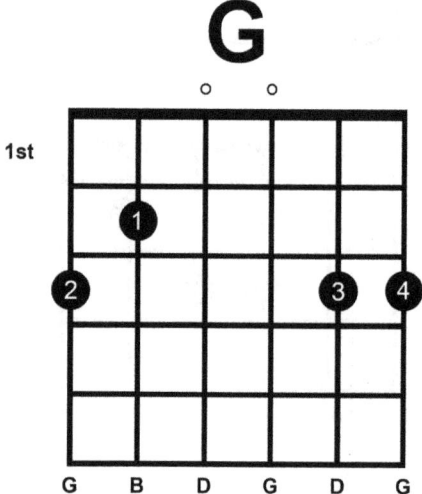

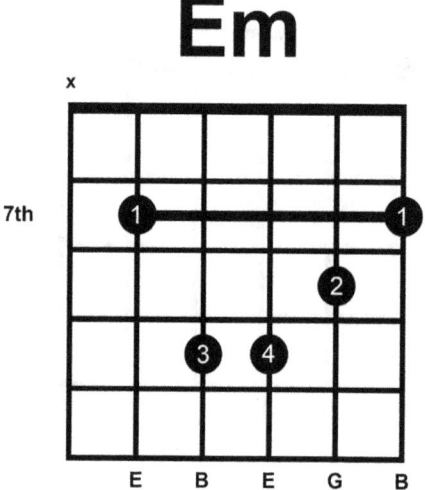

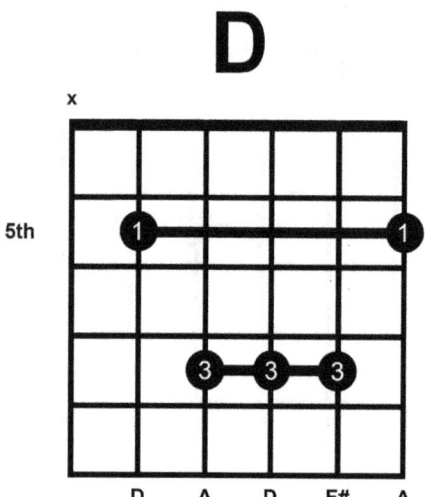

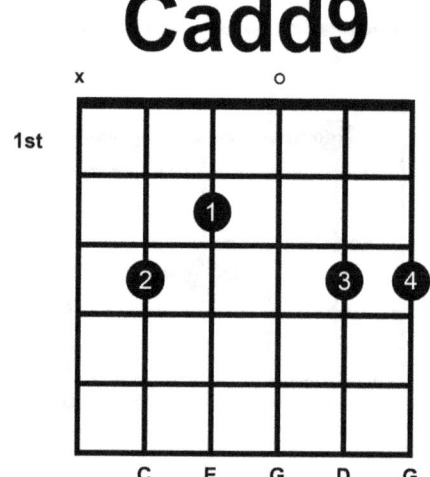

Summary

In this chapter, you've learned the essential chords in the key of E♭. Plus, we've walked through the practice of incorporating open and barre chords together for a unique sound. Finally, you've practiced the chords in the key of E♭. Next, we'll explore the key of A♭.

CHAPTER 5

The Key of A♭ Essentials

Introduction

Welcome to Chapter 5, where you'll learn the prominent barre chords in the key of A♭. You'll also practice your new chords with some fun progressions. The guitar lesson will teach you how to use a metronome, build speed and accuracy moving up the neck, and learn about rhythmic dynamic control. Let's dive in!

Key of A♭: 4 Flats (A♭, B♭, D♭, E♭)

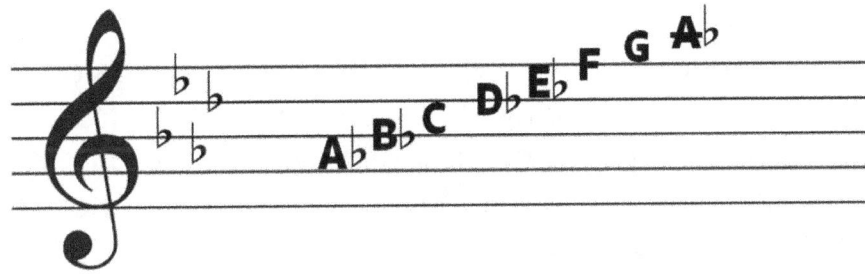

Essential Chords in the Key of A♭

A♭ Chord

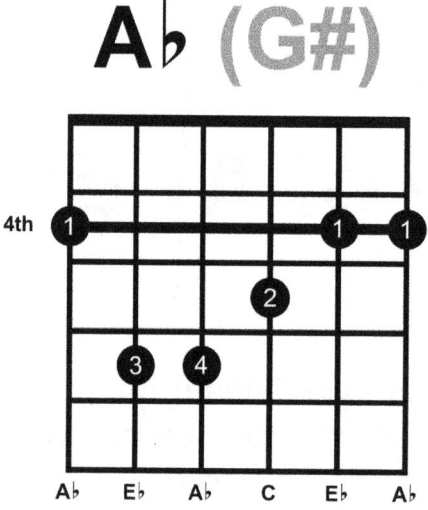

A♭ Chord Information:
- Number of Strings Used: Six (6)
- Level of Difficulty: Moderate

Follow this fingering progression to play an A♭ chord:

Begin by playing your index (1) finger across all six strings on the fourth fret. Then, add your ring (3) and pinky (4) fingers on the sixth frets of the fifth [A] and fourth [D] strings. Last, place your middle (2) finger onto the fifth fret of the third [G] string. Strum all six strings. Practice this chord to increase strength. Another way to say A♭ is G#.

E♭ Chord

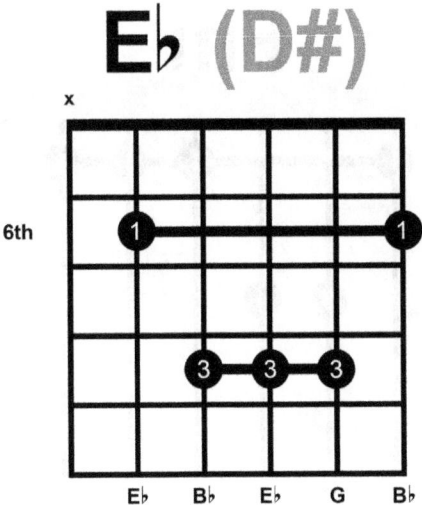

E♭ Chord Information:
- Number of Strings Used: Five (5)
- Level of Difficulty: Moderate

Follow this fingering progression to play an E♭ chord:

Begin by placing your index (1) finger on the sixth fret across the last five strings, omitting the sixth [E] string. Next, take your ring (3) finger and barre the eighth fret of the fourth [D], third [G], and second [B] strings. It is important that you do not cover up the first [e] string that the index (1) finger is currently pressing down on the sixth fret. Strum only the last five strings, omitting the sixth [E] string to play E♭. Another name for E♭ is D#.

Fm Chord

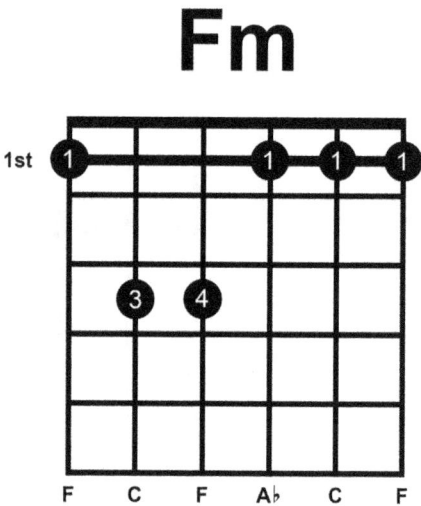

Fm Chord Information:
- Number of Strings Used: Six (6)
- Level of Difficulty: Moderate

Follow this fingering progression to play an Fm chord:

Begin by laying your index (1) finger across all six strings on the first fret. Next, add your ring (3) and pinky (4) fingers to the third frets of the fifth [A] and fourth [D] strings, respectively. Once each finger is in place, strum across all six strings to produce an Fm chord. Make sure to keep a strong barre on the first frets of the third [G], second [B], and first [e] strings. The minor note, "A♭", is created on the first fret of the third [G] string. Make sure you can hear that note.

D♭ Chord

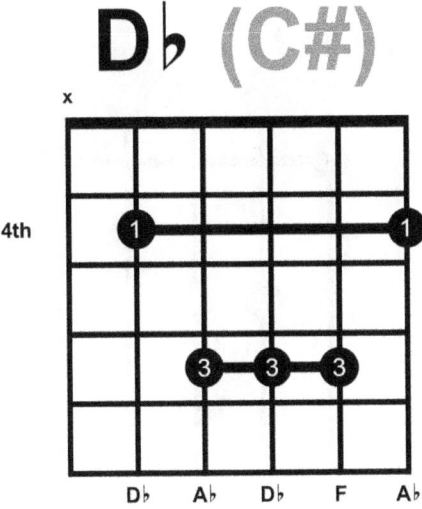

D♭ Chord Information:
- Number of Strings Used: Five (5)
- Level of Difficulty: Moderate

Follow this fingering progression to play a D♭ chord:

Begin by placing your index (1) finger on the fourth fret across the bottom five strings, omitting the sixth [E] string. Next, take your ring (3) finger and barre the sixth fret of the fourth [D], third [G], and second [B] strings. It is also important that you do not cover up the first [e] string that the index (1) finger is currently pressing down on the second fret. Strum only the last five strings, omitting the sixth [E] string. Another name for D♭ is C#.

B♭m Chord

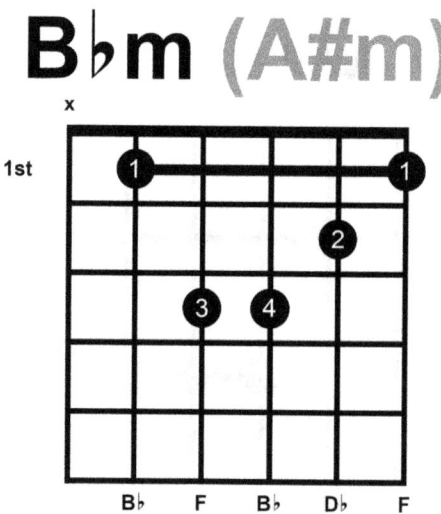

B♭m Chord Information:
- Number of Strings Used: Five (5)
- Level of Difficulty: Moderate

Follow this fingering progression to play a B♭m chord:

Begin by placing your index (1) finger as flat as you can across the first fret of all five strings, beginning at the fifth [A] string. Omit the sixth [E] string for this chord. Next, add your middle (2) finger to the second fret of the second [B] string. Last, add your ring (3) finger and your pinky (4) finger to the third frets of the fourth [D] and third [G] strings, respectively. Once all fingers are in place, you will strum the last five strings, leaving out the sixth [E] string. Another name for B♭m is A#m.

Practice

Now, let's practice your new chords learned in the key of A♭.

|: A♭ | D♭ | A♭ | D♭ :|

|: A♭ | E♭ | Fm | D♭ :|

|: A♭ | D♭ | Fm | E♭ :|

|: A♭ | B♭m | D♭ | E♭ :|

|: Fm | E♭ | D♭ | A♭ :|

Chapter 5 Guitar Lesson

Developing Speed and Accuracy

As you progress on the guitar, you will need to improve your ability to build speed and the accuracy of your chords. The following are some exercises to try using some of the barre shapes we've been developing together.

Exercise: Ascending and Descending Barre Chords

Throughout this book, you've learned six and five-finger barre chords. This first exercise works on developing your ability to move up the neck of the guitar using those barre chords. First, fret an F chord on the first fret. Strum the F. Now, gently let off some pressure, making the chord, and slide up to the Gb (F#) on the second fret. Strum that chord. Now, follow the same steps to move up one more fret to the third fret and strum a G chord.

Next, you need to find a metronome that will provide a consistent rhythm you can follow as you practice moving up the neck. Free metronome apps are available on smart devices, or you could purchase a physical metronome from online retailers or your local music store. Once your metronome is ready, set it to 65BPM (beats per minute) and press play. You should hear a prolonged and steady click count.

Now, go back to the F chord on the first fret. With the metronome counting off at 65BPM, move up the fretboard one fret at a time, moving each beat until you make it to the 12th fret. Then, come back down one fret at a time on the beat. As you get stronger at making these moves, increase your metronome's BPM. Using the six-string barre chord shape will help you develop skills moving up and down the fretboard.

You can also use the 5-string barre chord Bb on the first fret. Then execute the plan you did with the six-string F chord, but now use only the five-string version. Begin at the first fret with the Bb, move up to the twelfth fret one beat at a time, and then come back down. Increase the metronome's speed as you feel confident making each chord move.

Exercise: Rhythmic Dynamic Control

Let's add some rhythmic dynamic control to the mix using the same exercises. Rhythm dynamic control in strumming guitar chords involves varying the intensity and timing of the strums to create a more expressive and nuanced musical performance. For instance, if you strum the F chord strongly, strum the G♭ chord much softer and vary the intensity of the chords as you move up the progression. The benefit of dynamic control is that it adds emotional depth and variation to the music, making it more engaging and expressive for the listener. Practice rhythmic dynamic control using the six and five-string barre chord shape progressions learned in this chapter.

Summary

In the key of A♭ Essentials, you've learned the most useful chords in the key. You've used those chords to practice. During the guitar lesson, we've added ascending and descending barre chords to the mix while practicing rhythmic dynamic control. Now, it's time to move on to the key of D♭.

Micah Brooks

CHAPTER 6

The Key of D♭ Essentials

Introduction

Welcome to the Key of D♭ Essentials. In this chapter, you'll add new chords to play the fundamental chords in the key of D♭. Additionally, there are practice progressions that allow you to use these chords. Finally, the guitar lesson is about barre chords with extensions and modifications. For the first time, you'll learn how to strum part of a chord and use a single string as the bass note. Let's go!

Key of D♭: 5 Flats (D♭, E♭, G♭, A♭, B♭)

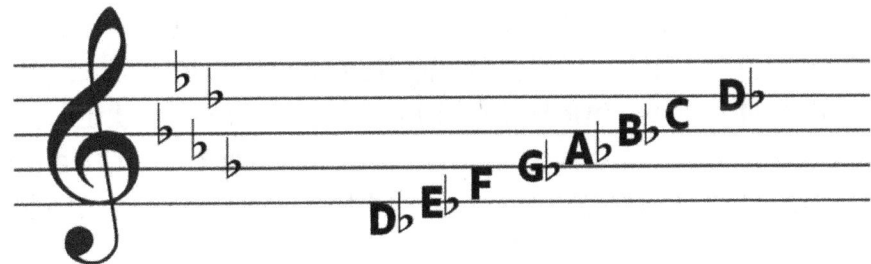

Essential Chords in the Key of D♭

D♭ Chord

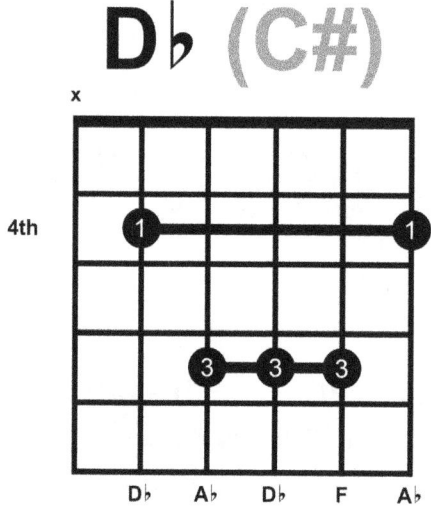

D♭ Chord Information:
- Number of Strings Used: Five (5)
- Level of Difficulty: Moderate

Follow this fingering progression to play a D♭ chord:

Begin by placing your index (1) finger on the fourth fret across the bottom five strings, omitting the sixth [E] string. Next, take your ring (3) finger and barre the sixth fret of the fourth [D], third [G], and second [B] strings. It is also important that you do not cover up the first [e] string that the index (1) finger is currently pressing down on the second fret. Strum only the last five strings, omitting the sixth [E] string. Another name for D♭ is C#.

A♭ Chord

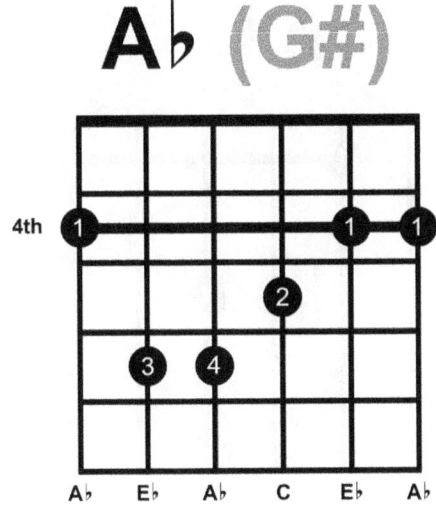

A♭ Chord Information:
- Number of Strings Used: Six (6)
- Level of Difficulty: Moderate

Follow this fingering progression to play an A♭ chord:

Begin by playing your index (1) finger across all six strings on the fourth fret. Then, add your ring (3) and pinky (4) fingers on the sixth frets of the fifth [A] and fourth [D] strings. Last, place your middle (2) finger onto the fifth fret of the third [G] string. Strum all six strings. Practice this chord to increase strength. Another way to say A♭ is G#.

B♭m Chord

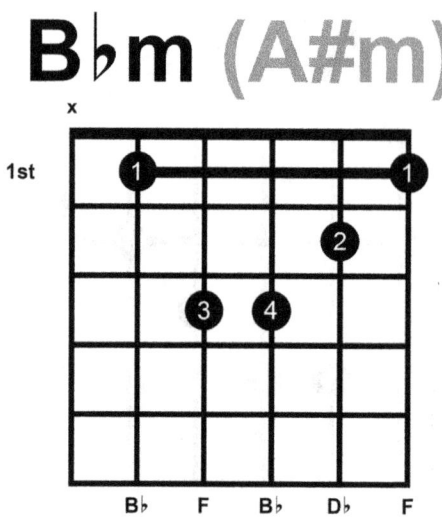

B♭m Chord Information:
- Number of Strings Used: Five (5)
- Level of Difficulty: Moderate

Follow this fingering progression to play a B♭m chord:

Begin by placing your index (1) finger as flat as you can across the first fret of all five strings, beginning at the fifth [A] string. Omit the sixth [E] string for this chord. Next, add your middle (2) finger to the second fret of the second [B] string. Last, add your ring (3) finger and your pinky (4) finger to the third frets of the fourth [D] and third [G] strings, respectively. Once all fingers are in place, you will strum the last five strings, leaving out the sixth [E] string. Another name for B♭m is A#m.

G♭ Chord

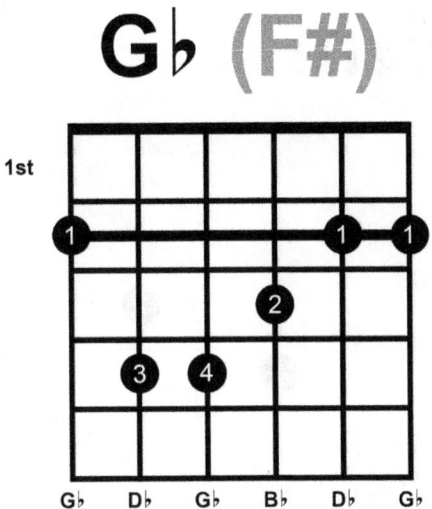

G♭ Chord Information:
- Number of Strings Used: Six (6)
- Level of Difficulty: Moderate

Follow this fingering progression to play a G♭ chord:

First, lay your index (1) finger across all six strings on the second fret. Next, add your ring (3) and pinky (4) fingers onto the fourth frets of the fifth [A] and fourth [D] strings, respectively. Finally, place your middle (2) finger onto the third fret of the third [G] string. Strum across all six strings. Another name for G♭ is F#.

E♭m Chord

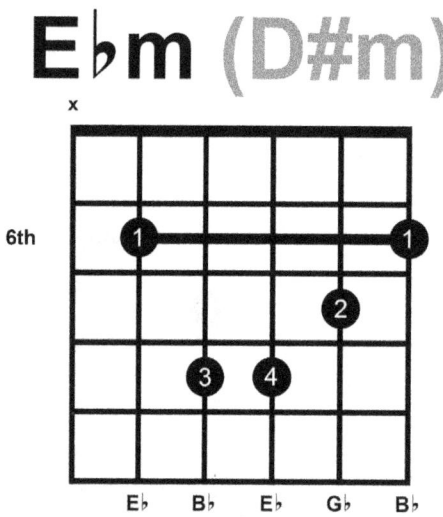

E♭m Chord Information:
- Number of Strings Used: Five (5)
- Level of Difficulty: Moderate

Follow this fingering progression to play an E♭m chord:

Begin by placing your index (1) finger as flat as you can across the sixth fret of all five strings, beginning at the fifth [A] string. Omit the sixth [E] string for this chord. Next, add your middle (2) finger to the seventh fret of the second [B] string. Last, add your ring (3) finger and your pinky (4) finger to the eighth frets of the fourth [D] and third [G] strings, respectively. Once all fingers are in place, you will strum only the last five strings, leaving out the sixth [E] string. Another name for E♭m is D#m.

Practice

|: D♭ | G♭ | D♭ | G♭ :|

|: D♭ | A♭ | B♭m | G♭ :|

|: D♭ | E♭m | G♭ | A♭ :|

|: G♭ | B♭m | D♭ | A♭ :|

|: D♭ | B♭m | A♭ | G♭ :|

Chapter 6 Guitar Lesson

Barre Chords with Extensions and Modifications

Thus far, we have strummed all the strings of the chords we have been forming. For instance, if we played an F, we strummed all six strings; if we played a B♭, we strummed the last five. For the guitar lesson in this chapter, we can modify the chord by strumming fewer strings or adding a bass note hit first and then strumming the rest of the chord. Let's dive in!

When you play an F chord with a down strum across all six strings, you invariably and briefly first hear a low F note from the first fret of the sixth (E) string. However, it is immediately less definitive to the ear because you hit the next five strings within milliseconds of that first F note. Thus, the ear adds all six notes together, creating the F chord. However, if you first hit the sixth (E) string sustaining that note alone for a beat, then hit the last five strings of the F chord on the next beat, you've sustained the same chord but have hit the bass note, F, on the first string, then the rest of the chord on beat two. If you follow that pattern for beats 3 and 4, you've created a rhythm pattern, separating out the bass note from the rest of the chord. Practice playing that pattern using the F note, then move up to the third fret to practice a G chord. You'll notice how your barre chords become more versatile as you can play multiple ways, one using all six strings at once and another with the bass note first, followed by the rest of the chord. You can repeat this concept using a B♭ chord or any other five-string barre chord you'd like.

Another method using a barre chord is to only play the last three or four strings. You will no longer hear the bass note in the chord, but it still stands out as complete to the ear. This is especially helpful when you play with a bass player. It allows the bass player to cover the low note and leaves you, as the guitarist, to only play the notes at the higher end of the spectrum. It's why when a bass player and guitarist join together, it sounds more full than when the guitarist is alone.

Summary

Throughout this chapter, you've studied the essential chords within the key of D♭. You've practiced some of the most important progressions. You've also learned how to modify your strumming patterns to include a bass note followed by the rest of the chord. That technique will be helpful in the future. Now, let's move on to the next chapter!

Micah Brooks

CHAPTER 7

The Key of G♭ Essentials

Introduction

Welcome to the second to last chapter! We are heading into the key with the most flats: G♭. In this chapter, you'll learn the key's essential chords and practice some of the most popular chord progressions. You'll finish understanding how to play some arpeggios on the guitar for the first time. Let's begin!

Key of G♭: 6 Flats (G♭, A♭, B♭, C♭ (B), D♭, E♭)

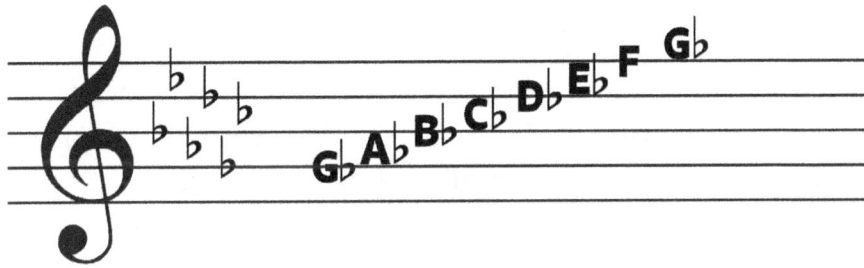

Essential Chords in the Key of G♭

G♭ Chord

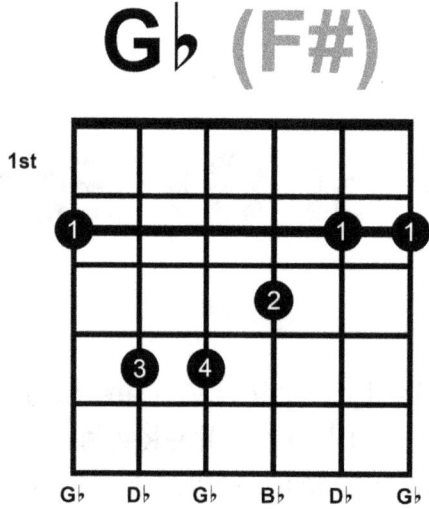

G♭ Chord Information:
- Number of Strings Used: Six (6)
- Level of Difficulty: Moderate

Follow this fingering progression to play a G♭ chord:

First, lay your index (1) finger across all six strings on the second fret. Next, add your ring (3) and pinky (4) fingers onto the fourth frets of the fifth [A] and fourth [D] strings, respectively. Finally, place your middle (2) finger onto the third fret of the third [G] string. Strum across all six strings. Another name for G♭ is F#.

D♭ Chord

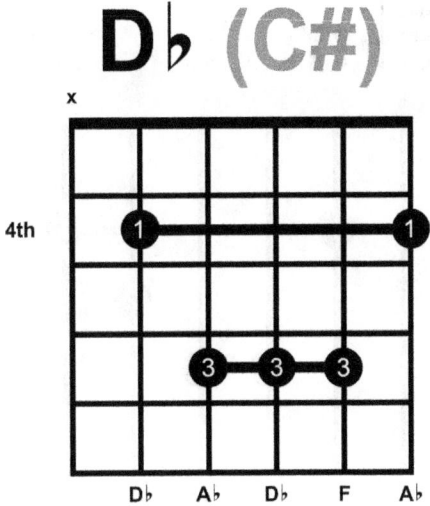

D♭ Chord Information:
- Number of Strings Used: Five (5)
- Level of Difficulty: Moderate

Follow this fingering progression to play a D♭ chord:

Begin by placing your index (1) finger on the fourth fret across the bottom five strings, omitting the sixth [E] string. Next, take your ring (3) finger and barre the sixth fret of the fourth [D], third [G], and second [B] strings. It is also important that you do not cover up the first [e] string that the index (1) finger is currently pressing down on the second fret. Strum only the last five strings, omitting the sixth [E] string. Another name for D♭ is C#.

E♭m Chord

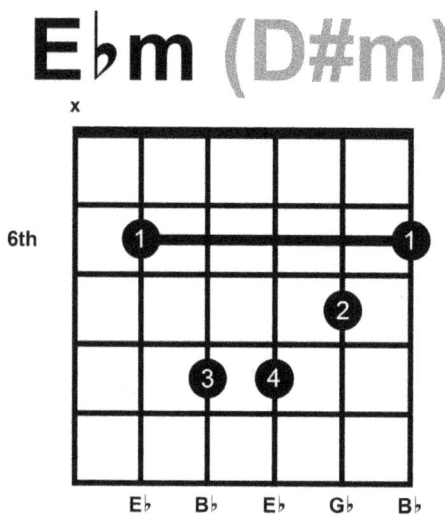

E♭m Chord Information:
- Number of Strings Used: Five (5)
- Level of Difficulty: Moderate

Follow this fingering progression to play an E♭m chord:

Begin by placing your index (1) finger as flat as you can across the sixth fret of all five strings, beginning at the fifth [A] string. Omit the sixth [E] string for this chord. Next, add your middle (2) finger to the seventh fret of the second [B] string. Last, add your ring (3) finger and your pinky (4) finger to the eighth frets of the fourth [D] and third [G] strings, respectively. Once all fingers are in place, you will strum only the last five strings, leaving out the sixth [E] string. Another name for E♭m is D#m.

C♭ (B) Chord

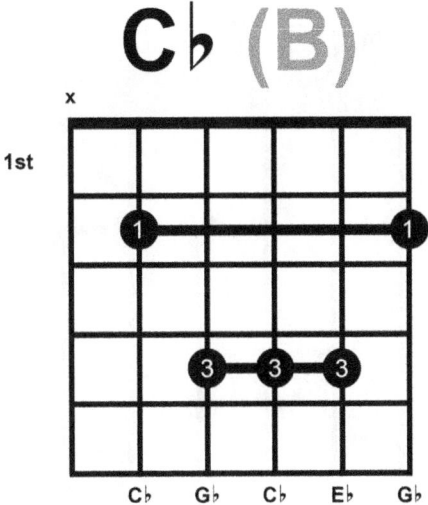

C♭ Chord Information:
- Number of Strings Used: Five (5)
- Level of Difficulty: Moderate

Follow this fingering progression to play a C♭ chord:

Typically, you will see this C♭ chord named B. However, in specific keys containing five or more flats, the C note is flattened to a C♭, allowing the B♭ note to exist as well without the need for two different notes using the note name B. Begin by placing your index (1) finger on the second fret across the bottom five strings, omitting the sixth [E] string. Once in place, take your ring (3) finger and barre the fourth frets of the fourth [D], third [G], and second [B] strings. It is also important that you do not cover up the first [e] string that the index (1) finger is currently pressing down on the second fret. Strum the last five strings to play a C♭ (B) chord.

A♭m Chord

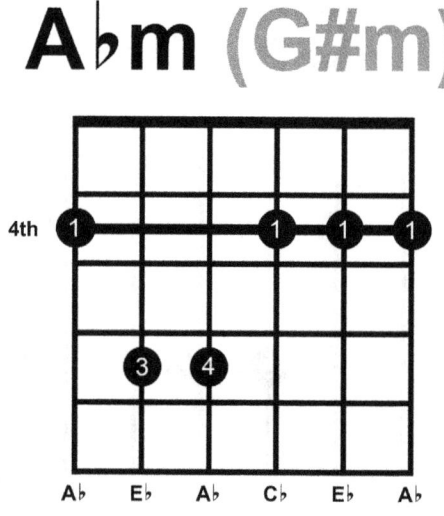

A♭m Chord Information:
- Number of Strings Used: Six (6)
- Level of Difficulty: Moderate

Follow this fingering progression to play an A♭m chord:

First, lay your index (1) finger across all six strings on the fourth fret. Next, add your ring (3) and pinky (4) fingers to the sixth frets of the fifth [A] and fourth [D] strings, respectively. Strum all six strings. It is essential to ensure that the third [G] string can be heard while pressing the fourth fret with your index (1) finger. That note is the minor note of the A♭m (G#m) chord. The other name for A♭m is G#m.

Practice

|: G♭ | C♭ | G♭ | C♭ :|

|: G♭ | D♭ | E♭m | C♭ :|

|: G♭ | A♭m | C♭ | D♭ :|

|: C♭ | A♭m | G♭ | D♭ :|

|: G♭ | E♭m | D♭ | C♭ :|

Chapter 7 Guitar Lesson

How to Use Arpeggios

In this chapter's guitar lesson, we will build on Chapter 6. Let's learn about how to arpeggiate chords rather than strumming them or isolating the bass note. An arpeggio is a technique where the notes of a chord are played sequentially rather than simultaneously. This approach makes each note distinctly heard, creating a fluid and melodic sound. Arpeggios add a new layer of complexity and musicality to your playing, providing depth and texture that enhance the overall expression of your music. By mastering this technique, you can bring out the full potential of barre chords, making your guitar playing more dynamic and versatile. Let's try some arpeggios now.

Let's begin by arpeggiating an F chord. Start by plucking the low sixth [E] string, then move to the fifth [A] string, the fourth [D] string, the third [G] string, the second [B] string, and finally the high first [e] string. Remember to sustain each note as you add them together. After reaching the high sixth [e] string, reverse the order, plucking the second [B] string, third [G] string, fourth [D] string, fifth [A] string, and finishing on the low first [E] string. Use a consistent up-and-down motion with the pick, ensuring each note rings clearly and maintaining an even tempo.

Now, let's try arpeggiating a B♭ chord. Form the B♭ chord by placing your index finger across the first fret, covering the fifth [A] string to the high first [e] string. Place your ring finger on the third fret of the fourth [D] string, your pinky on the third fret of the third [G] string, and your middle finger on the second fret of the second [B] string. Start by plucking the fifth [A] string, then move to the fourth [D] string, the third [G] string, the second [B] string, and finally the high first [e] string. After reaching the high first [e] string, reverse the order, plucking the second [B] string, third [G] string, fourth [D] string, and finishing on the fifth [A] string. Maintain an even tempo and ensure each note rings clearly, using a steady up-and-down motion with your pick.

You can use any of the chords we've learned as arpeggios. In fact, you could use the progressions above in the practice session as arpeggios. Arpeggiate each note of the chord, then move on to the next chord.

Summary

Throughout this chapter, you've learned the essential chords in the key of G♭. Additionally, you've practiced some of the most popular chord progressions. Lastly, you've learned what an arpeggio is and how to incorporate them into your playing. It's time to move forward into the last key we learn in this book!

CHAPTER 8

The Key of B Essentials

Introduction

You've reached the last chapter! Well done! Rather than playing in flat keys, we dive into a natural key with five sharps. It functions much like the flat keys, including mostly barre chords, so it is included in this book. You'll learn five chords, practice playing in the key of B, and know what modulations are and how to use them. Let's get started!

Key of B: 5 Sharps (C#, D#, F#, G#, A#)

Essential Chords in the Key of B

B Chord

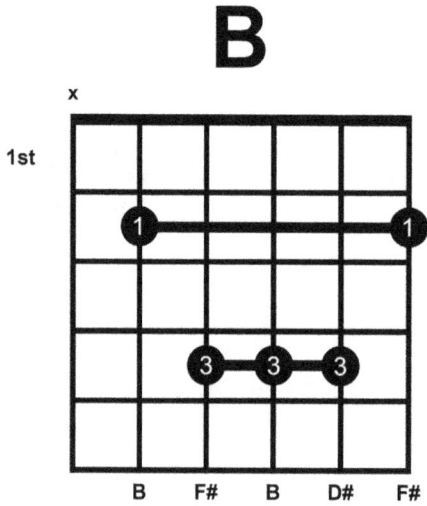

B Chord Information:
- Number of Strings Used: Five (5)
- Level of Difficulty: Moderate

Follow this fingering progression to play a B chord:

Begin by placing your index (1) finger on the second fret across the bottom five strings, omitting the sixth [E] string. Once in place, take your ring (3) finger and barre the fourth frets of the fourth [D], third [G], and second [B] strings. It is also important that you do not cover up the first [e] string that the index (1) finger is currently pressing down on the second fret. Strum the last five strings to play a B chord.

F# Chord

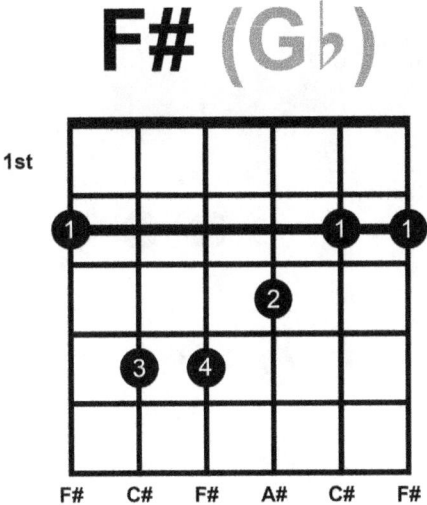

F# Chord Information:
- Number of Strings Used: Six (6)
- Level of Difficulty: Moderate

Follow this fingering progression to play an F# chord:

First, lay your index (1) finger across all six strings on the second fret. Next, add your ring (3) and pinky (4) fingers onto the fourth frets of the fifth [A] and fourth [D] strings, respectively. Finally, place your middle (2) finger onto the third fret of the third [G] string. Strum across all six strings. Another name for F# is G♭.

G#m Chord

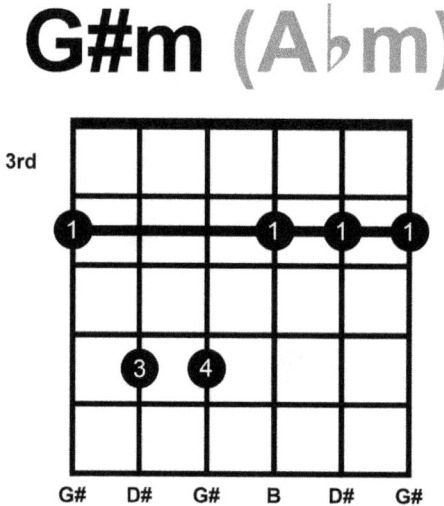

G#m Chord Information:
- Number of Strings Used: Six (6)
- Level of Difficulty: Moderate

Follow this fingering progression to play a G#m chord:

First, lay your index (1) finger across all six strings on the fourth fret. Next, add your ring (3) and pinky (4) fingers to the sixth frets of the fifth [A] and fourth [D] strings, respectively. Strum all six strings. It is essential to ensure that the third [G] string can be heard while pressing the fourth fret with your index (1) finger. That note is the minor note of the G#m (A♭m) chord. The other name for G#m is A♭m.

E Chord

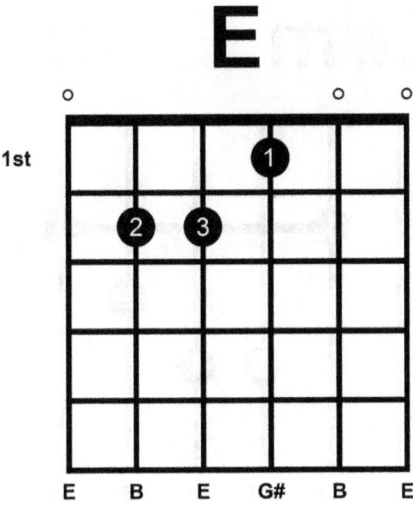

E Chord Information:
- Number of Strings Used: Six (6)
- Level of Difficulty: Easy

Follow this fingering progression to play an E chord:

Begin by placing your middle (2) finger on the second fret of the fifth [A] string. Next, place your ring (3) finger onto the second fret of the fourth [D] string. Last, place your index (1) finger onto the first fret of the third [G] string. Strum all six strings to play an E chord.

C#m Chord

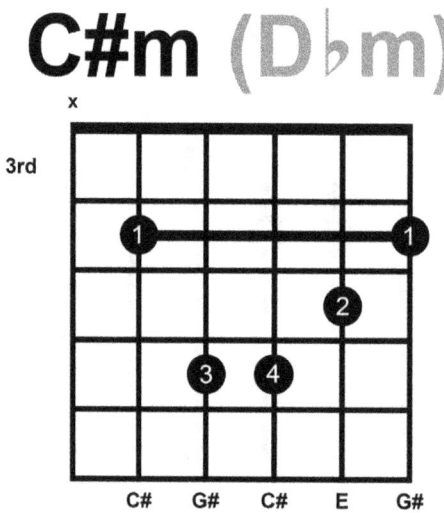

C#m Chord Information:
- Number of Strings Used: Five (5)
- Level of Difficulty: Moderate

Follow this fingering progression to play a C#m chord:

Begin by laying your index finger (1) as flat as you can across the fourth fret of all five strings, beginning at the fifth [A] string all the way across to the first [e] string. Next, add your middle (2) finger to the fifth fret of the second [B] string. Last, add your ring (3) and your pinky (4) fingers to the sixth frets of the fourth [D] and third [G] strings, respectively. Once all fingers are in place, you will only strum the last five strings, leaving out the sixth [E] string not being pressed down. The chord names C#m and D♭m are identical.

Practice

|: B | E | B | E :|

|: B | F# | G#m | E :|

|: B | C#m | E | F# :|

|: B | G#m | F# | E :|

|: E | B | C#m | F# :|

Chapter 8 Guitar Lesson

Key Changes and Modulations Using Standard and Barre Chords

Modulation, often called a key change, is transitioning from one key to another within a piece of music. It is a powerful tool in composition and arrangement that can add variety, emotion, and a sense of movement. There are different types of key changes, such as direct modulation, where the shift happens abruptly without any transitional chords, and pivot chord modulation, where a chord common to both the original key and the new key is used to transition smoothly. Understanding and applying key changes can enhance a guitarist's ability to create dynamic and engaging music, making it a vital technique in performance and composition.

So, let's practice some simple modulations from one key to the next. You'll hear a dramatic tonal shift as you shift keys. Our ears naturally recognize the notes to the key we are in. When we shift upwards or downwards in a key, our ears liven to the new sound and find the distinguishing changes. Here are some progressions for shifting only one-half step up with each modulation.

B to C to D♭

| B | E | F# | G | C | F | G | A♭ | D♭ | G♭ | A♭ | D♭ |

G♭ to G to A♭

| G♭ | C♭ | D♭ | D | G | C | D | E♭ | A♭ | D♭ | E♭ | A♭ |

Now, let's practice modulations shifting dramatically more by moving from one key up a third of the scale. Our ears find some similarities in the keys because they are relative to one another, which means they share some common notes. However, there is also a dramatic shift we recognize as well.

F to A♭

| F | B♭ | C | B♭ | A♭ | D♭ | E♭ | A♭ |

B♭ to D♭

| B♭ | E♭ | F | E♭ | D♭ | G♭ | A♭ | G♭ |

Summary

Congratulations, you've completed the final chapter! You've learned the essential chords in the key of B, practiced through some progressions, and used modulations for the first time. By completing this book, your arsenal of chords is immense. You're ready for just about any song you want to play. And you know the chords and techniques well!

Micah Brooks

CHAPTER 9

Final Greetings

You've made it!

You've mastered so many new and essential barre chords! Now you know the most commonly used chords in the keys of F, B♭, E♭, A♭, D♭, G♭, and B. Remember to practice for ten minutes daily, as regular practice is more effective than one long session each week. You're building callouses and developing muscle memory—so much is happening!

So, what's next? Great question! As you read this, I'm developing *Guitar Chords Three*. When it's ready, I highly recommend getting a copy to continue your journey with more challenging yet crucial chords. In the meantime, check out some of my other guitar books; they're a perfect intermediate step to keep you progressing. It's been a privilege to help you reach this point, and I look forward to continuing our journey together in the next books!

Recommended Resources

Guitar Chords One

If you happened upon this book before you read *Guitar Chords One*, I encourage you to grab a copy and learn the essential open chords that blend well with the barre chords you've just learned. In *Guitar Chords One*, you'll learn the foundational chords in keys like G, D, C, A, and E, along with proper guitar posture and positioning. You'll also explore smooth chord transitions, strumming techniques, and the use of a capo. This foundation is crucial for mastering the more advanced concepts in *Guitar Chords Two*.

Fast Guitar Chord Transitions

One of the neatest books I've written is *Fast Guitar Chord Transitions*. Most guitar manuals will show you how to play chords. This includes finger placement, which strings to strum, and so on. But, one overlooked aspect of the guitar is that transitioning between chords is as essential as knowing the chords themselves. While we have learned a little about this in this book, *Fast Guitar Chord Transitions* teaches a guitarist the steps of transitioning all the most popular chord moves you'll need to know. The book is arranged based on the key of a song you may be playing. It's worth every penny!

Guitar Secrets Revealed

Guitar Secrets Revealed is a book for the intermediate player looking for professional-level insights. Use this manual to get inside the mind of the pro. Find out how they think. You'll learn practicable, actionable music theory that you can implement today. Plus, find out how to use more unique guitar chord shapes that work like inversions of the essential chords you learned in this book. *Guitar Secrets Revealed* takes a guitar player to the next level–maybe even up to two levels!

Guitar Chords Flipbook

Guitar Chords Flipbook is a book that fits in your guitar case. Inside, you'll find more than 100 of the most essential chords with diagrams and written step-by-step finger placement suggestions. Treat this book like a Swiss Army knife. It is a reference manual that is intentionally small and goes with you as you perform. Check it out!

Piano Chords One, Two, Three, and Four

Like the *Guitar Authority Series*, I recommend my *Piano Authority Series* of books: *Piano Chords One*, *Two*, *Three*, and *Four*. Written much like a manual, you'll learn the most essential chords on the piano and how to play many versions of them. If you've ever longed to be able to play songs on the piano and accompany yourself as you do on guitar, these four books will help you do that. Grab a copy of each and see what you can accomplish!

About The Author

Why so many people learn music from Micah

Micah Brooks is a seasoned music educator and author known for his engaging and personalized teaching style. With over fifteen years of experience teaching guitar, ukulele, piano, and music theory, Micah tailors lessons to each student's pace and interests. He believes in guiding students to take that extra step in their musical journey, fostering creativity and exploration.

I've taught guitar, ukulele, piano, and music theory courses for over fifteen years. In fact, that's why I've written seven books for guitar, one for ukulele, and four for piano to date. My emphasis has always been, and will likely always be, in commercial music. While I think classical music is worth studying, I always find myself improvising over the original melodies–even those of the greats, like Beethoven, Brahms, or Bach. It's human nature to explore or be curious, and I love teaching with the mindset that the music greats of the past are like proven guides. They shouldn't always be copied, but rather those from whom to learn.

Living twenty-five miles from downtown Nashville, TN, has provided me and my family privileges in music that I'm sure are not given in every town. You can't throw a stone in Nashville without hitting someone who is personally or has a family member in the music industry. Not one of us takes the Grand Ole Opry backstage tour because we plan to be there as music artists someday. Even if we sing and play music for Jesus as Christian or worship artists, we likely won't spend the time or money on that tour. We plan to perform on that ageless circle that lands center-stage someday ourselves.

My wife is wonderful and my greatest joy. We love our four kids, who keep us very busy and quite exhausted! We also have two energy-filled dogs!

It's an honor to help you unlock your musical potential. Let's make music together and discover the joy of performing with others.

Blessings,

-Micah Brooks
www.micahbrooks.com
Find me on Facebook, Twitter, LinkedIn, Instagram, and Amazon.com

Connect With Micah Brooks

Please share this book with your friends

If you would like to share your thanks for this book, the best thing you can do is to tell a friend about *Guitar Chords Two: Barre Chords* or buy them a copy. You can also show your appreciation for this book by leaving a five-star review on Amazon:

www.amazon.com

Sign up for Micah Brooks emails to stay up to date

Subscribe to the Micah Brooks Company "Stay Connected" email list for the latest book releases. This email list is always free and intended to deliver high-value content to your inbox. Visit the link below to sign up.

www.micahbrooks.com

Contact Micah

Email Micah Brooks at micahbrooks.com/contact. I want to know who you are. It's my privilege to respond to your emails personally. Please feel free to connect.

Follow Micah Brooks:

Facebook: @micahbrooksco
X: @micahbrooksco
LinkedIn: Micah Brooks
Instagram: @micahbrooksco
Amazon: amazon.com/author/micahbrooks

If you have trouble connecting to these social media accounts, please visit www.micahbrooks.com.

Guitar Chords Two

www.ingramcontent.com/pod-product-compliance
Lightning Source LLC
Chambersburg PA
CBHW081339090426
42737CB00017B/3215